King Baby

ALSO BY LIA PURPURA

Stone Sky Lifting (poems)
The Brighter the Veil (poems)
On Looking (essays)
Increase (essays)
Poems of Grzegorz Musial: Berliner Tagebuch
and *Taste of Ash* (translations)

LIA PURPURA

King Baby

Alice James Books

FARMINGTON, MAINE

10 9 8 7 6 5 4 3 2 1

Alice James Books are published by Alice James Poetry Cooperative, Inc., an affiliate of the University of Maine at Farmington.

ALICE JAMES BOOKS
238 MAIN STREET
FARMINGTON, ME 04938
www.alicejamesbooks.org

LIBRARY OF CONGRESS CATALOGING-IN-PUBLICATION DATA
Purpura, Lia
  King Baby / Lia Purpura.
    p. cm.
  ISBN-13: 978-1-882295-68-5
  ISBN-10: 1-882295-68-4
  I. Title.
  PS3566.U67K56 2008
  811'.54—dc22   2007044644

Alice James Books gratefully acknowledges support from the University of Maine at Farmington and the National Endowment for the Arts. ❧

Cover photograph courtesy of Alan Kolc.

Jed. Again.

CONTENTS

ACKNOWLEDGMENTS

Many thanks to the following journals where these poems
(sometimes in earlier versions) first appeared:

Pebble Lake: "Once I was walking in the cold...", "Remember your
home...", "There was a frozen moment...", "Then: leaves. For
covering..."

Witness: "Whose need is this: I take you from cold...", "Warmth
is coming. The air is almost violet...", "King Baby, are you
singing or asking to be fed?..."

A thrill of gratitude to whom it may concern—
and to Joseph, for finding.

Once I was walking in the cold
and the light
kept leading, leaden
leading, leaden like a chant
for snow to come and knock out
school for another day.
I was talking with my friend
when my child interrupted.
With much effort he called me down
to fish the emptiness that would become
his brother from the river.

No stylus touched you.
No router, but a sharp blade
precisely made your mouth.
An awl worked on the vertical
and a threader, a contraption
like fine fingers, for the embellishment
of eyes and voice. Work took place
at night while you neither slept
nor woke, and were not yet, King Baby.
Through your open mouth now
one has a clear view of your spine.
The story of your creation starts
with a force that wanted something
and worked to see if you were it.

Decide for us
the most powerful force,
remember, we ask not expecting
love or *time* or *water,*
or that you'll even speak to us.
Speak to us. Is impatience a force?
We're waiting. Remember
who found you.

Granted that day to us:
the sight of you,
your refusal to end
by collapse or shattering,
incongruent body
round among the jagged rocks
and frozen trickle,
round and going on
so much so that
in the forest without us,
did King Baby, alone and fallen,
make a sound? is no question
to pose to a child.

King Baby, tire me
as you see fit,
as you see I am fit
for constancy (all those
hours of night feeding).
Let what you've seen of us
decide our fitness,
judge even the youngest,
his love, in your sight, judge
how he lifts you out of the river,
jumps across and grows suddenly tired
of climbing the banks with you
slowing him down
then hands you over so I, too,
might be tired:
forgive how he shares with me
everything he loves.

Now that I have what looks like everything,
I thought I'd put my yearning aside.
What is the source of our wanting, King Baby,
more than enough butter for our bread—for who
among us can use, in truth, the word *bread*
to mean exactly the sustenance one needs? How do you
want more, ever more, and love the unending desire
that hollowed you and left you a body adorned,
by whose embellishments you were found, set down
on this, our tree-lined bank, washed up on our shore,
the trees' black, all-around breathing
a festival by a river.

You with a block of ice in your head,
a block in your stomach, a skirt of shells
and shells for eyes, leather ears,
wide mouth eliciting such tenderness,
face down in the stream
then carried through woods
by one (I will ever be your subject)
who took the long way home
through a grove of bamboo
and thawed your head body spine
in a bowl otherwise used for soup—
thus dissembled and known,
now can you rest?

You came to us
on the coldest day
cut loose and far from home.
We thought you were
a buoy in the ice.
And what were we
before you arrived,
how did we live
knowing nothing
of you? How did I,
who said at first,
leave it, it's nothing.

Furnace of Charity, Rose of Patience,
I never learned such formal appeal,
but here, will try:
Oh, roadside aster of emptiness,
hope of rot, a thing in need
of shelter too, oh, lion of ditchweed,
patient in ice, King of sudden
recognition, animal piss, crashpad of chance,
risen among gourds, dried, gutted and cut.
Sighted (dark irises of crimped shells) and given ears,
Baby found among the tangle, dried
and set upon a shelf, the crack in your head
lit in the early light of promise,
and again at nightfall, so that your white spine
carved and smoothed,
is a filament, scepter, sword conducting us all . . .

Remember your home.
With your frozen cowrie
eyes to the riverbed,
remember warmth, the scent of grain,
start telling
and you won't be able to stop.
Up you go. Go on. Remember
the box and the packing,
the light, late afternoon
through a rough slat, so blue.
Remember for us
the landing and shore.
Tell how the river
took you, and the story
of the four swallowed
bottle caps. Go back
to the lathe, go back to the knife.
Remember our footsteps
towards you.

There was a frozen movement
in the tender shape of—
I believe it was a shapeless
tenderness, the way it moved
under the ice, like blood under
a microscope, with a heart
like nothing we knew
but recognized
for its pushing against its contours.
When we stepped on the ice
it shimmied, extended,
let's say an arm, the way it reached,
or cheek, the way it showed the force
of holding back breath.
This went on in a theater, contained,
a show so we might see,
through darts of ice, pools of thaw,
how a thing that cannot be touched
moves to fill an emptiness
so much beyond its body
that it imitates a prairie
and there comes a little song
with popping and snapping
to accompany it.

Then: leaves. For covering
the lashed, rattling shells,
for covering your voice.
Then: water pooled
a hard shelf into your side.
Now: lean against a window
with stubborn paint splatters.
Lean sea-facing, where you were
headed, where piecemeal
you would have sifted
smaller than an eye could find
through the water's mesh of rocks,
as, look—there's skin
of milk carton going by,
flesh of fish pared
to shine. Left there,
you'd have made
a very brief song.

There's always a reason.
You make the reason or don't
understand it. But reason comes
pouring. While your body
looked like a buoy, we were part
of a calm understanding.
Then we saw *you*.
Popular thought went crazy:
we must have found you
for a reason!
Forgive us such arrogance:
why wouldn't we be *your* reason,
your shapely passing thought,
raw moment's explanation?
And when we parted the branches
and late afternoon sun striped down,
why wouldn't we be
odd light come to the planet
just for you?

Am I equal to a thing I'm given,
a thing that you'd make meaningful
by simply leaning up against it:
ivy in here, unbloomed
pussywillow out the window,
scraping at the house?
What, at my back, is scraping
and scarcely heard;
to find it, would closing
and pressing one eye help?
Or two, which causes an inward
falling-into-dark where
the cliffs really are,
the blind, reddening stars
in the never-truly-dark
of the contemplatives, where
shine, like sun on a bottle cap,
finds a small thing,
and caresses it for the sake of nothing?

A stone, hit, brightens with a hammer blow
and pocked stars come to the surface.
I know at least to pray
for my unquiet heart,
for the brightness to be released—
though by *brightness*
I mean many competing things.
I want to be of use and with a task:
a rubber band, a strawberry
with months of sun under its
pierceable skin. A piece of type
in a printer's case, an O
to double as nothing in a pinch.
The race track of a paperclip.
Like a fork, like a candle, a glove
to glove a hand in cold, I want
to fall into particular use.
I want my heart to be an awl.

Now, rescued,
you have elegant designs to interpret,
theories, lapses, salvage operations
of all sorts, all yours. Welcome. And love
so bracing you may not get your
shells to echo properly in its presence—
love's raw berry, bursting,
late sky's orange ribbon
pressing a blue stain, down.
And though my love is not a sweet
subsiding, reduced to a thin, sharp lozenge,
your throat must be aching with it by now.
Love burning throat back to spine.
That's the feeling I meant.
Come sit with us and eat.

King Baby, what did you bring,
what did you keep from the other world,
you without pockets, with a mouth fit to swallow
change in rivers, glass, pebbles—
let us place one object at a time
on a plate, please, to examine.
How to read your expression in this,
a strange land, mouth a quarter-orange
wide so our river, eddying around you
might fill you, weight you where
you lay. And was there weeping
when you remembered plains, mountains, grasslands?
And did the weeping become a current here?
Your leather ears, stiff now from soaking,
are they meant to make you more precisely
resemble us? That you might hear and attend us?

Unable to otherwise pray,
I can always apologize—
sorry if the house is a trap,
sorry you'll never see a barn,
ocean, mountain range, prairie.
It's very stormy here.
A storm's good green is ruching up for hail,
and where you would be
is getting hail, too.
I mean, where we found you.
Remember, just this morning,
the sky arranged such a bright, capacious spell—
where you were before that I don't know.

There is a leaf dangling on a tree
like a flag, shredded. A tatter.
It distracts. It dispels myths
about giving up for the greater good
and it being time to go. It's nervous because
I am. I match the face of it, a scrap in wind.
My lips are sore from all this pursed thinking.
What do you sit with alone, King Baby?
What are you waiting for?
There is a red just past the tree, and all the other trees—
it's a bent something. A red
something in snow. A kid's,
crumpled on the ground.
It must have fallen.
I can't see exactly.

If you want a field defined,
I'll show you a field. Out any window,
really, is a field, its darknesses
and slopes called hillocks, its burrs
and saw grass whistles.
Matter of habit with those I love,
or might, to show them the field.
Bring up the nature of
ever-falling into it,
falling daily, falling faster, steepness
in the motion, or
we can hold it with one eye shut,
in the window here, a square of it,
its square heart bursting. I think
the heart of a field must always hurt,
postage stamp-sized declination,
root form, much divided
by morning, by evening, by our visits.

Someday you'll understand speed,
and why, when you're happiest,
you'll still want angry music.
To know the word "cudgel,"
look into your body:
a short stick used as a weapon, a club,
and, *to take up one: to debate,*
and also *the act of thrashing:*
there's music for that,
and times of day when a window
darkens and becomes a mirror
so you might see for yourself
how we lifted you
up from the river, over our heads
and also the room where the story's told
again and again (*buoy,* we thought,
then *instrument,* then—)
and how upright you are, jaunty
with that little tilt, as the tale goes on.

Are you hungry, King Baby? I haven't even asked.
There are two of us in the kitchen tonight
and you are not one of us.
I toss a stone from our conversation into air.
I think it's one you held in your body,
what the river fed you, hospitable
in the way of a river, since, really, our
conversation goes something like a river,
offerings carried along and some thrown
right into the center where the current
is fast and goes like gold
finches turning into light—at one angle
they're erased, at another they're green,
greened from within. Was the green
expressed by a braising light?
Does it glaze them,
as the conversation turns, is glazed too,
and darkens, and deepens?
It's late now. We've been at it for hours.
Don't go looking. I'll leave you this
whole plate of crumbs.

Was there a special silence in the market
when all the tourists left?
Was the silence there below
the dirty cloth draped over you and others,
and did it bring the country back,
and all the country stories? Here the tops
of trees above you are called *crowns*.
Here you fit our hero's profile:
all you have to do
is fall into a ditch, a mine, a river,
and wait to be found—
though at home you, among many, waited,
assessed by all the roving eyes
of those who picked you up, considered you,
but found instead real bone dice, cups carved from native trees,
flat-faced dolls with necklaces, things easier to carry
than you, King Baby.

But let me tell you my favorite story—
the one where the true king is disguised
as a beggar and he wanders the countryside, is hurt,
maybe falls into a river and is found,
carried to a simple home, and tended,
and not because he is a king—it's that
the decency in this story can't be bought.
I like best the silence in the story, and the cold—
when the king is put to bed
under the best quilt in the house,
and the poor man also goes to bed, but on a pallet on the floor,
and believes he'll wake
to an ordinary day.

Best you know my hands
which, by asserting here some order,
took you from your discontent
at being nowhere (as I call it,
since I was not there)
and cleaned inside you, scooped
from your belly the junk you swallowed
to constitute your body
as it was in the beginning.
I took and laid your parts
to dry before the coiled radiator.
If you thought these gestures were extinct,
think again. Here: I give you
Nabokov, holy in his way, whose
acts of precision purify and surprise,
and who I read without stopping,
straight through until exhaustion:
The spiral
is a spiritualized circle.
In the spiral form, the circle,
uncoiled, unwound,
has ceased to be vicious.
It has been set free.
I work with the hands of one who first made you.
I work slowly to retrace the gesture,
though now there is, from such a journey,
a crack at the back of your head.
I turn it to the wall,
so through your mouth,
it looks like a stitch of lightning.

King Baby, many things go by
I want to tell of:
that plastic bag, crumpled
and rifled by wind so resembles
a hurt pigeon, I can hardly
walk past without stopping to help.
And yesterday, the orange halo
burnt around a leaking battery shone;
a little shelf of ice hanging over the gutter
cracked when I pressed it, and made the sound
of a box shutting, a shoebox, some barest,
smallest breath and echo in the store
I stopped to listen to.
The ice was opaque, very fragile, and below,
the melt was running. I could hear it, but it was hidden,
like a red bird in a red place is hidden.

Bells for morning open up the city,
open morning's yellow, tender
underside, and the far off
flashing lights on TV Hill
line up along the dark branch of an ash
so the branch seems to catch,
even on a day as cold as this.
The book I'm reading,
reckoning with, is *recking* me,
which meant once: *to mind, to heed.*
I tell you this, who see me daily undone,
whose whittled spine is an arrow up
to a rustling thought—a humming,
a radiator's hiss, mourning
doves, or wind through eaves,
a blue-windowed attic folding night in—
a thought, muffled, the way
a steam-gash cut in pie helps contain
everything inside, opening a bit
so some pressure escapes and things firm up.

I thought I saw you in the museum
of things gone terribly wrong,
the museum where I tried all day to make
the babies there not real.
Whose bleached or sepia'd heads crested
the terrible solutions, who floated
upright in their jars below the meniscus
slung between two worlds.
By the circular jars and squared-off jars, I sat down
to be with one and, sitting, saw it
was two, one's grimace, one's tired
eyes closed, joined in the middle.
Their wheat chaff, lightest, barest,
feather eyebrows. The hair,
real hair, in little grassy tufts.
I counted the mistakes I made—
calling one *it,* taking pinkness for health;
someone else counted
the forty-six twists in their shared umbilical cord
and wrote the syndrome on a card,
and turned the backs and heads just so
to make the gaps there visible.
I resorted then to ancient thinking
about holy anger, the Devil's hand,
striking a mother straight through to her child.
I didn't end that day with thanks.
It was not gratitude that rushed in.
It was no relief at all to think of you,
mostly whole, only a few wide cuts
and little breaks I know of,
where the sun enters.

Know that in the museum
there were blades with handles of mother-of-pearl
and the silk of long use was a light upon them,
there were files as thin as saw grass,
tinctures and phials of amber poison and silver mercury pills.
A visitor's lip curled at a blood-rusted bandage.
A visitor's eyes turned from a carbuncle in plaster.
Know that when I hit the wall
of skulls, I learned that at one time
calipers measured for dark thoughts.
What did a dark thought look like then?
They checked many sailors', convicts', kidnappers'
skulls to locate a dark thought's
origin. And after that
it got very complicated to measure . . .

Here are some distinctions I've been thinking about:
grief and sadness, and the rift between
the dramatically used "weeping" and more familiar "crying."
Then too, I have these skulls to boil up, a fox's, a raccoon's.
I'm keeping them next to the nests until
I find the right pot, large and deep enough—
then I'll arrange them
clean and white along the sill
and stand back and listen: grief or sadness?
Which best articulates the bones'
sharp edges and hollows?

Today I learned many people
swallow bones, bone shards, and slivers
that turn to arrows, saws,
awls in the stomach and have to be removed.
In their black velvet cases,
labeled with numbers in the museum,
the bones told about
finding a way, staying an irritant,
fleck in the eye, but darker and deeper—
splinter of the original animal
wanting back in to all that flesh.

I was working on an idea about a God
upright and unconcerned
with all the heavy fate surrounding you.
I was almost finished, but then I saw
concern, our finding you a form of it,
and I could believe in the heart and the odd words
that gather around it: *fist, muscle* and *pump.*
I could believe in the body. That we could travel
far together. Past billboards. Past road junk.
To rest stops that, at first, are nowhere,
like the places ants map out with those
lines they make of thought, of an idea
so good, so uninvented,
some roving part of original thought
they listen to, sniff, know what to do with.

Tell about the music before you left,
and how your body
falling and rising, went marrying
moment to moment. I think
to drive wishes and paper petitions
into the fire to singe and curl
or onto the water to drift
takes a music wholly without cleverness.
Only desire. Only accompaniment.
Your music is loosed as a pulse of white birds
inside a chest wall.
That sound goes very deep when you're shaken.
May I use your body too?

I will try it your way
(that famous look of distance)
but how to hold my body
on a morning when a jay
flies so close to my head the air
splits and I hear the gash
or gasp of my own breath.

I will try to stay
beside an absence, sit beside
the opening that is your mouth,
which is older, darker, greener
than the ivy on the sill.
I will try by thinking of the jay,

who for the sake of hunger
dipped down and tipped in
not knowing what it wanted,
who tried and came close
and, last minute, came closer.

Once I crashed hard
and came eye to eye with the street.
That space
between eye and street
was quiet. And lit.
Never was the sun so much mine I thought.
Was it true? Or in trying it out on the tongue,
was that a better way of saying,
as I say now in your presence,
I am not alone.

Who wouldn't want to be so marked by sun?
A radiance beginning just below the waistband
pushing up and warming—
but already it's late in the morning.
I should have risen earlier.
To the angle of light holding you that day:
all gladness. For gladness I should have risen earlier.
I should have risen to see you in the prevocalic light,
as it was before we found you. I should have risen
right after the dream: someone marked my back
with a sunrise so loud, so intentionally yellow,
with such strict beams, it made the opposite of everything
also true—the dark, front, northside of me patched with snow.
And all day I had to stay doubled like that.

Sometimes I hold you, and holding
think you're warming.
Sometimes in a clutch, I want you explaining,
as if the scent of your wake were not enough.
And you're noisy. If I shake you even gently
your many tongues slip into mine,
that I might hear your voice in my head.
What do you want me to hear?
Holding you, I am held
entire as a branch in wind
that might snap, or lift a bird as easily.
Either's fine, don't ask which will come?
You mean, I should know an occasion when I see it.

An amber horse has come along.
Stay next to it on the shelf, this glue-eyed thing
sun catches and runs through. It's a gift.
It's an occasion to talk about love.
Look closely.
Gaps are in the way. Ground swells.
In sharpest light
look straight through the horse's perfect, shattered,
brown and yellow form.
Tell me everything
about peaks and rifts contained.

Come. It's my birthday. Make me over
into a thing a tree could use, like light, to drink.
Or a drink so lit by thirst
it assembles like a river at its birth.

This morning a shadow
made an indigo bunting
of a burl in a tree.
I did not know where to turn—
to the hawk
and the sight of its red tail going,
or to the blue thought
that couldn't be.

Dim light, King Baby. All the better
to sketch the tale (first tale,
best tale) of how you came to be with us.
Over and over the children want
the drama by the river.
But look, I say: right here is coruscated
light on windows and pampas grass
to harvest in the fall. Habituation
comes and goes. Shadows and hachures
make flat things stand right up.
I do not draw well, but to hold a thought.
Get comfortable, I tell them. Here's my picture:
a man on a ladder hammering up a satellite dish,
with a neighbor below watching him work.
Kids don't get the weirdness of perspective
and ask: why is the man on the ladder
so much smaller than the neighbor?
Well, in this picture he's far away and when
people go away or high up
they get smaller so the mind can see the plan.
To make up for the distance,
it seems that you can hold them in your hand.

The thorn I found today was not unlike the carved, raw
pick of your spine. The thorn I found I used
to pierce a note intended for a friend.
I wanted to show him Bosch's Hell and so wrote down
see color plate 80 and "The Temptation
of St. Anthony" which also is pretty hellish.
I picked it up not believing it was a thorn—
so much thorn, so virulent a thing.
I pushed it just a little, against the inside of my wrist,
then I sailed it through the paper.
I thought about what it broke from—
the whole of that,
how clean and white the break.

Your form is always with me as I walk,
empty and pierced. Today I stopped to see,
and touched by seeing, sparrows in the bittersweet,
deep in a copse of thorns,
their bodies soft among the sharpness,
indigo, in that light.
Not mottled-slate. Not bluish-grey.
How good to find distraction
in precision.

To every simplicity I've ever known: bye.
Sometimes I want to be seen as ornament.
Sometimes I come down in the morning
to stand in your piloting gaze.
I am unnerved. I am adoring. Sometimes,
like any animal, I act beyond the confines of my nature.
Though wary of simplicity, I can be pleased
by sun on a rough wooden table—

but the shells that jewel your body, and how they use
your emptiness for speech—such deft and noisy tools!
What do I put on and wear best? A simple
gray sweater. And yet. And yet.
The simple reduces juggling to arrangement.
The simple tethers event to event to event.
The simple maxim *Use it up, wear it out,*
make it do or do without burns a log
and makes of ashes, soap. Please, no,
and not a plank worn smooth.
I want to be the rough lip before efficiency,
to require multiple attempts,
to scent the air as you have
with your large presence and be found
as you have been found, King Baby,
implicit in the landscape as a flaw, a buckling,
a sinking fast, the carelessly carried forth.
Oh, let me be odd in my surroundings.

Sorry you tilted, just now, into ivy —
it must have been our jumping, all our leaping,
imitation ferocity. Even while playing,
brief bursts (they come, midday—like love
and can a body hold it all)
knock me down, too.
I think you came from a place with a poultice
recipe for everything. And people
threaded needles—is it true?—in one smooth gesture
cleanly through the eye. And knotted up
the tail which held the whole line fast
as it slid into the ragged tear
that hopping fences always makes.
King Baby, set upright once again,
my child's game is over. Quiet reigns.
He must be reading now. Far off, somewhere.

If not for some essential need,
we wouldn't have been walking there that day,
and come to find a bank,
a gully, roots and tangled
blackberry by the trickle—
would not have seen
in the barest trees, evidence: wind,
the invisible, being made not-so. Then you.
At home, you rest beside the ivy
in a place more wildness wants to know—
and so I use a form that orders distance. *Thou.*
Oh, cordial, sturdy belief
there is somewhere
we have not wholly touched.

Let me confess—I don't believe
things happen for a reason.
I believe we bend events around to meaning
or recline with them and mystery at once.
I think we say things happen for a reason
if we don't believe the making is important.
But it is. More so than a reason from on high,
come to clear a path, and shine a light.
It can't be the reason's known
by someone, some force, and is bestowed.
What mind would leave the atmosphere,
its feel and crosshatch out,
that we might never sense a thing unfolding?
And suffering-as-meaningful, I cannot abide.
But making something in the moment that suffering subsides,
in that time, with bits of wood, a hollow gourd,
stones, bottle caps and light, the sharp cold,
a red bird's black beak in a crack of ice,
sipping—let that stand for holiness.

Sighted: a red bird (not the robin) returning—
so what to call that moment?
Given: changing light, late March,
the ice-shelf in your belly long since thawed,
the rain barrel after last night's downpour, overcome—
what's that? And the erratic flight
of a dun brown bird making up for plainness
with looping, dizzy speed—
I think it's my turn to say what that means.

You are the one I want to tell:
I have a perfect thing, and many impulses toward it—
keep it. Look at it. Sometimes turn it when
the light's just so and want it even more—
or want more from it. It's not a bloodless, stony thing.
It's more a ruby with stacked-up rooms
and I can see doors, even wedge
a few open and wander in and out, at will.
Caressing glints. Fingertip along the glint
so each sharp corner paints its inner chamber
wilder still. Imagine in there, too,
skeins of milk-blue peridot, scrims of ouzo
warming, tipping—what is having
even more of a beautiful thing?
If deep in a cave, it's so dark you can't see,
what does *going deeper* mean?
Here is a ruby in a plain, brown world,
rough and held in its brown rock.
It could be cut away. It could be
stripped and finely planed, and set.
But there's that little wall, that boundary
whose fault line says
to love it best, don't.

You were the brown of a mottled orange
I used once to make a pomander. I stuck
the fruit with cloves and hung it
with a ribbon from a light.
I made staves and belts of cloves
contain the color
and the room was lit with scent.
Attended, you, too, warmed—
tea stain, sun on inner arm,
a chestnut's shine, shingles
weathering in sun, in rain,
in hail, in all modesty you became
one-who-shows-it-on-the-skin:
here I fell,
and here, on this smooth part, I didn't.

Yesterday I heard a guy say his first film
was either spoof or homage, he didn't know which.
Why couldn't he tell?
Two thousand years ago
the Greeks thought crystal was water frozen
so hard it couldn't melt. They didn't know
but took a guess (those jagged edges so like ice
in every way, except)—and then they let it rest.
An imperfect, but good try.
You know our story, King Baby, and how we guessed
about you—buoy? Plastic thing? A mess? And now
there's everything else you've become to add in:
thing before which I cannot hide.
Occasion. Companion. Object
of desire. Homage is a street
lit up by declarations,
a thronging street where I am
touching each shell's perfect shine
and bending in the light that holds you
on the sill late afternoon, light you wear
like an air of certainty.

Those people who feel lucky every day—
who are they? Casting for good
in the spiked arms of a dark pinecone:
Oh, the fragrant seeds in there! they say.
Like teardrops, I say. *No, as fat as grains
of rice!* A maggot, I say. *No, a scar
that's healed and holds a story ever after,*
or *a pastille, tusk of ivory, forest
entirely rolled and sealed!*
On the subject of gray, I say
pigeon wings unfurled, the color of
day after day rain and flooded basements. *No,
remember, our pigeons live in trees
and freely on the roofs of houses,
not packed in Ionically or Dorically downtown.*
What would you say, King Baby,
to a very crook-necked squash: Exodus 3:5:
The place on which you stand is holy ground?
Or as Nabokov wrote of a dying moment,
*I recall a particular sunset—it lent
an ember to my bicycle bell*
to emphasize flare over loss?
So close to you, the volatiles, the inerts
and elementals line up right here in the pantry:
the best experiments begin at home. Start with
the common, everyday: NaCl under a microscope.
See, they'd say, *the caverns bloom
and light slides down the necks of crystals!*
Me? Today? I'd say add water. Stir.
Kiss the homemade tears away.

The idea of a flounder's eye
migrating up, I learned,
recapitulates
all that is probable about evolution.
For symmetry, one eye slips over
to meet the other. The skeleton changes,
underside pales, topside alters to match environment.
Then you come in, in the middle of a thought:
your toothless, ever-open mouth (a flounder's
toothless, too) your white spine ever-visible,
your shell eyes ever-open, each holding
a tiny sea-surge.
Here, right now, out the window
what do you see, King Baby?
I see the tallest pussywillow
in the neighborhood, blooming slowly,
a worn silver bucket, a ficus tree,
a pile of dull-white asbestos shingling—
asbestos in its natural form is
fine-spun, cottony, a composition
caused by heat, deforming pressure, shearing stress.
I learned all this in a museum.
That was its own journey. Let me bring it all home:
I want to see as you do, King Baby.
I know I'm always asking, asking, asking,
but when I'm walking in the city
and the skyline is interrupted,
I want to know how to cast my eye up.
Let it linger on blue.
Let the roar come.

I went out for a walk to find a blue boat
to remind you of home and having to go
beyond the known. I did not find a boat,
but more blue things than I thought abound.
A chip of CD, some spray-painted grass
where BGE plans to dig.
Little Sam's pen cap, a bit of tarp
with the rivet still in like a tired, open eye.
One stripe on a drinking straw
in brown grass—I may have to *make* this boat, I thought,
but then, oh, the blue Parthenon on a rained-on coffee cup,
a blue bucket swing. Recycling bins. Blue coffee
stirring stick and Bud Lite pack. A blue Dum-Dum
wrapper, condom, wire. Slate bits.
Gum. Cobblestones. Schist.
And so many things that didn't apply—
an orange reflector cracked in two,
a flat lipstick, the silver pond of a crushed can in sun.
I thought a blue grocery bag might be it, then
spur of the moment, crossing the street
towards snow drops (not blue but notable),
almost home and still without a boat,
a weathered chair came up,
the wooden slats just the blue I was hoping for,
dusty, peeling, the white below leaking its cool dust through,
the slats not nearly thick enough to use to carve a boat—
but I'll bring you by and you can rest your eyes there,
sit a moment, propped among the waves of blue
that so nearly knocked me out, coming as they did
when I thought I couldn't make a thing for you.

I saw today the way a pigeon,
using only the available
air, light and angle, remade
itself for long seconds
into a red-tailed hawk.
I know a hawk is bigger
and its call is all hard-edge,
(a disadvantage, you'd think,
making prey hide from it—
it makes *me* want to hide,
and every muscle in my back go taut)
but the pigeon banked
and used the low morning sun
to light its wings, to push off from,
and there it was, sun against
the body of the bird, lifting
and flaring until I saw
the red that wasn't there,
wings grow confident,
and air believe it all.

I regret that I have used,
cannot believe I used as solace
It's only going to get worse.
What's that supposed to do—
supplant a current misery
(I know you miss your faraway home)
with future, super, mega doses,
thus rendering present sadness,
distance, loss, less potent?

And if I say
Welcome, big silver train-wreck-cloud
of seventeen-year cicadas,
making the woodborer, who ate a tunnel
through our top step a mere annoyance—
its hole just ugly, not a hazard, not to worry
that the kids pour potions down it
and the concoctions run along
some hidden path and sit there,
vinegar and baking soda
frothing away the stair's soft core—
if I say *welcome,*
what's that supposed to mean?

It comes to me, amid all the abundance:
I almost passed you over.
I almost said *No, leave it there whatever
it is*—brown bag of air, round, frozen
melon left from summer.
I almost didn't dare.
Often I assemble myself
back at the beginning, beside
your simple promise:
if you pull me out, then . . .
It was not spoken. If it was,
I would have flown to it, I would have
been an eschatologist of the worst order,
reading groundswells, star charts, daybreak
for *then what, then what?*
I do not want to know the end,
your end, my end, oh, keep me from it
and from knowing what you promised
(though I think it's blooming).
Let me remember:
my son's arms couldn't reach
so I took over. I pulled you out
and held you dripping very close,
while everyone waited
to see what the air and light, just after a promise,
an old, old fable reconstituted, looked like.

Where was I going
before all the trees,
breathing and fallen,
made, with the river,
the day I'm in now
and the tasks it requires:
pick up this jewel,
gaze on this mess.
Stay on the banks
of the story
unfolding.

Whose need is this: I take you from cold,
settle you in, find you a light, window, home.
For corollaries see *flowers*: sun comes, and rain,
and those are things a flower needs.
But even a perfect system looks
unbalanced after a while—
what about what *sun* gets
from a blazing poppy?
What about rain's unseen *ascent*?
Have I understood Nature at all correctly—
is it possible *you* chose *me*?
And not because I'm good
(I melt the ice, I prop you up)
but because no one else would do:
my flare, thin skin, dark center.

The question of those purple blooms
being weeds or flowers is upon us once again.
It's a question of desire: if you want them
that's one thing; if they just appear
without your hand, another.
I was out for a walk
when the tight clustering along a garden gate
made them look like things from an era
of simple pleasures.
For days after I saw them,
last thing before sleep and first
when I awoke. Then this came back:
in Warsaw where I once lived,
on a cold afternoon, on the way to the tram
at Broniewskiego
I saw a chimp running down the sidewalk.
Everyone saw it. No one moved.
Everyone watched until the chimp
found a doorway and stopped to rest—
like anyone would for a moment
out of the cold, spring wind.
No one was running after him.
On the same street, in another doorway,
an old woman was selling purple bouquets,
perfect for a tiny vase;
she lashed the blooms together with dirty string.
Weed or flower, pulled from the same dark,
with bound stems, I bought a bunch
and held them like the others did,
as was the custom, sensibly, blooms down,

those blooms picked anywhere along a road.
What were they called? What did I get?
King Baby, before you had a name,
before I took you home, I held you like that.

Warmth is coming. The air is almost violet
with browns and greens parting for early crocuses.
My acts feel heavy where, hand over hand, spring
is climbing, raw-recruit style
into air, where much yellow pollen hopes.
I hope. I wait for morning to come. Poor sleep
with its offerings I refuse. I rise and touch the pampas grasses
and steady myself. I study my inner arm,
striped by a slat of dawn or moon, and live there for a while
in the calm of not-knowing.
I think there are some questions about forgiveness to attend.
Like when transgressions are overturned
by luck or circumstance
and forgiveness is not required—
isn't it still required?
I mention this to you, King Baby,
because once, I heard the first bird at 3 A.M.—
and alone as I was, forgive me, I cursed it.

The cherry blossoms hurt.
Why is that?
Their tender gold centers
are misting with pollen, speckling black
in light rain. I keep hearing
"The Song of Cherry Blossoms"
I played on recorder as a kid
and was told all the kids in Japan
were playing on little violins.
At the same time, I thought.
There was no absence then,
not like this. Not the sky uncolored,
cold spring, wet, with black crows
and brashly, the cherry singing backup—*no,*
no, no, stay on the path.
Pass us and cover
yourself with your wing.
You are too big
to light in our branches.

I think I'm getting ready for a death.
All the (word, frighten me) *candidates* step up
and I push them back. I'm rough in my treatment,
though I see why they would come forth:
One smokes a lot.
One drives very fast and dreams of a crash.
One often gets a needle-stick.
My grandmother's very old.
Why, in spring?
All things whistle through your wide mouth, King Baby.
I once told someone I loved
say it into my mouth and I swallowed the words.
Where'd they go?
They lived for a while like wood smoke,
and moved like cool water over impediments.
Sometimes I overhear my son playing:
If you're small enough you can follow and
No one gets out of here without dying.
But this was more formal.
I don't understand where those words went,
except deep in my body.
Love said those words.
Someone is dying.
Do I hasten things by saying?
Am I that terrible child?

King Baby, I know your hollowness
and the way you sing when shaken.
If I am shaken
by the pink and white falling
tea cups of magnolia,
pink weeping cherries,
how would my song sound?
Dotting a lawn, sotto voce
and up from the past,
something in meter,
in French, in Greek, all come back
to me while fleeing?
When I'm out walking
and someone runs past,
always, always in their wake
I breathe deeply.
I want whatever, unbidden,
they give me.

King Baby, are you singing or asking to be fed?
Does need, like a pine tree, grow a knot at each limb's tip
and from there spring an arc of spikes—an explosion
held against the sky (the sky not blue, just white, this cold,
   late spring)
the needles conducting, the loose,
reticulate ends charged, alert, attentive—
such need! You sent yours out? Kept yours in?
I see into your mouth, cut wide like a ditch,
it's as dark as night fallen, or morning unrisen, I can't tell which,
but there, all the red's contained in black,
and back of the throat, I hear it decided: song, and not hunger.

14.95
5/08

ALICE JAMES BOOKS has been publishing exclusively po-
etry since 1973. One of the few presses in the country that is run
collectively, the cooperative selects manuscripts for publication
through both regional and national annual competitions. New
regional authors become active members of the cooperative,
participating in the editorial decisions of the press. The press,
which historically has placed an emphasis on publishing women
poets, was named for Alice James, sister of William and Henry,
whose fine journal and gift for writing went unrecognized within
her lifetime.

TYPESET AND DESIGNED BY CHRISTOPHER KUNTZE

Printed by Thomson-Shore
on 50% postconsumer recycled paper
processed chlorine-free

RECENT TITLES FROM ALICE JAMES BOOKS

The Temple Gate Called Beautiful, David Kirby
Door to a Noisy Room, Peter Waldor
Beloved Idea, Ann Killough
The World in Place of Itself, Bill Rasmovicz
Equivocal, Julie Carr
A Thief of Strings, Donald Revell
Take What You Want, Henrietta Goodman
The Glass Age, Cole Swensen
The Case Against Happiness, Jean-Paul Pecqueur
Ruin, Cynthia Cruz
Forth A Raven, Christina Davis
The Pitch, Tom Thompson
Landscapes I & II, Lesle Lewis
Here, Bullet, Brian Turner
The Far Mosque, Kazim Ali
Gloryland, Anne Marie Macari
Polar, Dobby Gibson
Pennyweight Windows: New & Selected Poems, Donald Revell
Matadora, Sarah Gambito
In the Ghost-House Acquainted, Kevin Goodan
The Devotion Field, Claudia Keelan
Into Perfect Spheres Such Holes Are Pierced, Catherine Barnett
Goest, Cole Swensen
Night of a Thousand Blossoms, Frank X. Gaspar
Mister Goodbye Easter Island, Jon Woodward
The Devil's Garden, Adrian Matejka
The Wind, Master Cherry, the Wind, Larissa Szporluk
North True South Bright, Dan Beachy-Quick
My Mojave, Donald Revell
Granted, Mary Szybist
The Captain Lands in Paradise, Sarah Manguso
Pity the Bathtub Its Forced Embrace of the Human Form, Matthea Harvey